LOVE,
IMPONDERABLE
LOVE

First Printing, 2024
by Off-Trail Publishing
PO Box 656
Harpers Ferry, WV 25425
USA

Cover photo: Nancy C. Ross

Love, Imponderable Love: 100 poems in 100 days Volume II
Print ISBN: 979-8-218-16695-3
eBook ISBN: 979-8-218-16697-7

Also by Lavinia Lord
*What Would Love Say Today? 100 poems in 100 days
Volume I*

LOVE, IMPONDERABLE LOVE

*100 poems in
100 days
Volume II*

LAVINIA LORD

Off-Trail Publishing

To the love in everyone's heart.
Speak up! I want to hear you.

Contents

Contents ~ ix

Contents ~ xi

Gratitude

Carla, what a gift of an editor you have been, with your keen eye for detail, your English teacher savvy, and your love as a dear friend. I felt so well supported with your company in this process.

To my parents and my lineage – thank you for this rich and miraculous gift of life. The vivacity with which you lived yours inspires in me a fullness of heart.

To my sisters, Johanna, Lucy, and Julia – we are as different as the four seasons we were born in, and I'm grateful for what I've learned from and with you, growing up together. Merci pour tout.

To the HeartMath Wednesday Heart-Lock-in crowd of souls, guided by Steve and Gail in this past year... Hillary, Carolyn, Lindsay, Jessica, Donna & Donna, Silvia, Mary, Catalina, Lucie, Sherry, Susanna, Cathryn, Ron, Erin, Sharon, Hannie, and so many more. Thank you for co-creating the space to experience what it's like to "move more love through your system."

Miss Jenny, what a ride this has been, and thank you for your kind, heartfelt, steady friendship throughout.

Nous continuons, chère Muriel, à retrouver la beauté et les rires, et pour moi cela a une valeur formidable.

A las Queridas Elementas – Bea, Ana, Mónica y Amaia, las siento muy presentes conmigo en esta exploración de lo que es vivir en Amor. Me dan esperanza que todos podemos brillar al mismo tiempo con alegría, placer, satisfacción y armonía, alineadas con el universo cuántico. ¡Qué regalo más rico!

Preciosa Vane, me has abierto un mundo de confianza con dimensiones que nunca imaginaba

fueran posibles. Muchissimas gracias por tu acom-
pañamiento mágico, potente y amosoro en este
último año.

Bless your inspiring and energizing infusion
of pleasure into leadership, decision-making and
healing, Carley. In the time leading to this book, I
have harmonized and balanced my inner feminine
and masculine loves, thanks to my work with you.

Aaah, Kristen, I thank you for the model you
live in being true to yourself and for the support
you have given me to find my way through the
layers of illusion to my core presence, as I learn to
listen to my own heart.

Allie, thank you for your bravery and willingness to keep exploring the inner wilderness together. Blessings for your beautiful path.

Captain Bill, thank you for your friendship
and wisdom in this realm of recovery and re-
discovering one's self. They wound their way into
the poetry in grounding ways.

To the Creative Alchemists – Phyllis, Sarah, Jillian and Laurie, for the many in-depth explorations of creativity and expression.

So much gratitude to Shahida Arabi, Lisa A Romano, Dr Les Carter, Dr Ramani, Melodie Beattie, Marie-France Irigoyen, Ariel Leve, Stephanie Lyn, and so many more for your brilliant work in co-dependence, narcissism, gaslighting, people pleasing, and everything related. You have contributed powerfully to my sanity.

To Lara, Brian, and the MOSAIC Project, for the peace-building skills, the love, the hope and inspiration you continue to instill in the kids and the expanding MOSAIC community.

Gracias Ross, my parallel brother. What an inspiration you are when it comes to loving life and living large.

To the darkness and light within and without that give us the wholeness of who we are. Thank you for the balance and for the illumination and expansion of perspective.

Thank you to the natural world – for the simple and intricate lessons you offer freely through your beingness and unquestionable authenticity, guiding us back to ourselves if we are willing to be honest and open.

To David Whyte and his Many Rivers team – the lively conversation continues, and so does the sincere gratitude.

I am grateful to the Shenandoah River (Beautiful Daughter of the Stars) and the Potomac River (The River of Swans) for the gift of integration, which came through while living at their confluence.

To Love, where would I be without you!?

PROLOGUE

The first round of 100 poems from Love in 100 days (30 May - 6 September, 2020), though initiated by curiosity, began in fear, distrust and hyper-vigilance. I was deeply guarded, scared to open. I thought I had to give or do something in order to receive love. I resisted my feelings, judging them all as wrong or impermissible. I was afraid even love would reject me, not understanding that I was the one who had been rejecting myself.

The context of the second round, resuming only two weeks after the end of the first, remained similar – imposed isolation, dysfunctional social systems – both collective and personal, tragic human and natural disasters, distressing polarities, 'isms' of all sorts, painful relationships, and distorted perceptions of love. Present also was the momentum in social justice, healing collective and ancestral trauma, as well as growing curiosity in the capacity and intelligence of the human heart. Parallel to my own inquisitive experiment, I continued to be inspired by John Lewis's way of nonviolence and the "graceful heart." (Lewis, 77)

> *We are talking about* love *here. Not romantic love. Not the love of one individual for another. Not loving something that is lovely to you. This is a broader, deeper, more all-encompassing love. It is a love that accepts and embraces the hateful and the hurtful. It is a love that recognizes the spark of the divine in each of us, even in those who would raise their hand against us, those we might call our enemy. This sense of love realizes that emotions of the moment and constantly shifting circumstances can cloud that divine spark. Pain, ugliness and fear can cover it over, turning a person toward anger and hate. It is the ability to see through those layers of ugliness, to see further into a person than perhaps that person can see into himself, that is essential to the practice of nonviolence. (Lewis, 77)*

Interestingly, though the external context was similar, *I* felt different. More present. More hopeful. The daily consistency of listening for that larger love was laying a foundation. I continued with David Whyte's invitation to "connect to the feeling and write from there." I don't know if those are his exact words, but I learned the idea from him. After first trying it with Grief, I unfolded this whole experiment from that simple, deep process – extending the open invitation to Love.

On this second 100-day journey into Love's wilderness, I wanted to move beyond the path less traveled and go off-trail altogether. Starting from a higher place inside, I noticed this time from the get-go I was looking for beauty, for what felt good, for comfort. I was looking for the love in my own heart, and surprisingly, I was starting to find it.

My level of trust in love's reliability had increased over the first hundred days because, no matter what I felt or experienced, by the time the poem came out, I was always met with grace, and always felt understood. I started to recognize the emergence of a voice that was gaining more confidence and that felt like mine. The comfort of authentic expression increased, and with this new-found inner ease, the time it took for me to shift out of self-judgment and into curiosity shortened. As a result, this reassurance opened access to deeper layers. My scary insides didn't frighten me as much, the depths were less daunting, and the truth became a relief. Self-destruction turned into self-compassion. I discovered I could trust my emotions too, and that they could serve as a navigation system for me.

So, in these next 100 poems, I experienced a greater awareness of old conditioning as illusion, and a more intense emptying out of anguish, rage, guilt, and other heavy emotions, resulting in an unfamiliar void. I landed in an unexpected sense of emptiness. Eventually, the fearful dread of what I might find inside shifted to anticipation of the love and clarity that came through in the poetry. I felt an opening to new horizons. I discovered an imagination that expanded differently each day.

Sometimes the poems were from a specific situation or interaction with a particular person. Other times though, the emotions just spoke for themselves, making up metaphors to express themselves more clearly. Sometimes I didn't know where the pain came from, or who "they" were.

Each emotion had a different character. Fear and anger had many flavors. Some emotions melded better together, like resentment and fury, or gratitude and joy. Others, like ease and fear or doubt and faith, couldn't coexist. Like magnets, these emotions attract more of the same, while repelling their opposites.

I noticed that the word "friend" often came out in the poetry, and that it wasn't always related to specific people, but rather it was a feeling underlying the word – a feeling of trust, relaxation, mutual respect and inspiration. The word "friend" encompassed a whole range of beings, including emotions, family and strangers, that shared a common feeling of peaceful connection and geniality. Through this process, I learned to be a better friend too.

The crumbling of old rigid fixed patterns, revealed new openings to unforeseen possibilities. And the phoenix that came forth from the ashes in the first round transformed into the singing and playful presence of the Skylark after the second.

In the last month of her life, just six months ago, I asked my mum how she would define love, and she paused in silence, then shook her head. "It's imponderable," she answered. As this echoes my own experience with these poems, in her honor, I named this second volume of the experiment to get to know Love, "Love, Imponderable Love."

Welcome to volume two...

FROM: LOVE #101

Wednesday, 30 September 2020

My Sweet, you're back!
So good to find
a brand-new track –
a higher ground
to start this round,
A broader base
to keep you safe,
A wisdom wealth
to bring good health.
The more you hear
the more it's clear.
The truth you see
Has set you free.

FROM: LOVE #102

Thursday, 1 October 2020

It was no wonder that
swift stormy winds
ushered you off the island.
"Go on!" they declared.
Blowing from the South
with warmth,
they eased your way North.
Upon arriving
to Moosehead Lake,
the first clear spot of blue
in five days' time
appeared in the cloud-filled sky,
initiating the clearing
to later offer you the first
blanket of stars

since you left home.
The thick dense fog of the island
had stayed put, giving way
to this beautiful autumn
crispness that shone
bright colors across the
sunny blue clear morning.
You have found another haven.
A safe refuge of clarity
and hope,
allowing a return
to the essence of Love.

FROM: LOVE #103

Friday, 2 October 2020

Onward you go, into the unknown,
moving to new rhythms that speak
the true language of your beating heart.
And although Divine flow
feels effortless when you're in it,
the fear of the shift looms,
as you wonder how the illusion
of old structures will continue
to fall apart.
The closing of the chapter floats
parallel with the gorgeous leaves
of Autumn falling from the trees.
Maybe painful Goodbyes can still
be beautiful.
But despite the trepidation,

with each step forward
you land on firm ground and are met
with warmth and welcome.
Each time you open, the path
unfolds with a new twist,
and you find yourself at the edge again,
but now, instead of being alone,
you're with friends – some
old, some new – all
expanding...
because now, in your new existence,
you're starting to see
what it is
to BE
a friend.

FROM: LOVE #104

Saturday, 3 October 2020

Basking in the golden light,
a flicker of warmth
makes its way through the
cold crisp Autumn air
as surfers brave the chilled waters,
finding their own connection to flow,
wave after wave.
You do the same in
opening to this beautiful day.
You too will surf,
wave after wave
in chilled waters,
mindful of the undercurrent.
Deeper down, the YES
brings you a hot cuppa

and a tasty hot breakfast,
and sends you on your way.

FROM: LOVE #105

Sunday, 4 October 2020

Even if your voice feels tiny here,
I still hear you.
Even if old pain lingers,
it's of the past.
Even if resentment rises up,
it's from collapsing patterns.
Even if you're surrounded in this moment,
you're not crushed.
Even if you're stressed,
you can still breathe.
Even if it smells bad,
you don't live here.
Even if you didn't sleep,
you're strong enough for today.

Even if you're wondering, "why?"
I still love you.

FROM: LOVE #106

Monday, 5 October 2020

Home again,
where rest gently holds
your aching heart
and you find your own
place to breathe
in your center,
easing back into
expansion,
and reclaiming the beauty
that emanates from
your core, as a blessing,
not a curse.
Your raw nerves are
soothed by your
flourishing plant friends

that continue to grow
new shoots and flowers,
and the Malibu couch
that welcomed you
into evening stories
the night before.
Here you are, learning
to let go,
so that grand-scale creativity
can play with synchronicity
and guide you on your way,
as John Lewis would say,
to "love in action." (Lewis, 78)

FROM: LOVE #107

Tuesday, 6 October 2020

I feel your estranged self
as though lost afloat
in an ocean of guilt,
fearing that if you
grabbed the tiller
to steer towards the shores
that call you,
you would be betraying
your own blood.
But the blood that flows
through you need not
carry the weight
of those before you,
and instead, can
serve to heed and honor the

healing, past and present,
so essential, yet
dismissed as though
you are the problem.
Stay true to your
Good compass as you
gather the courage
to sail your own vessel.
Dive inside the deep pool
of LOVE that bubbles up
from the abundant
source, and, wet with joy,
set your colorful spinnaker
to catch the support
that will fill your sails.

FROM: LOVE #108

Wednesday, 7 October 2020

Back to the drawing board,
you reconnect
with your aspiration,
since your imagination
is just waking up,
and visions of the future
are still blurry.
But you know what freedom
feels like in your cells now,
and that is enough
to maintain hope.
The external explorations
guide your focus and
steer your faith,
and the internal garden

anticipates your
careful tending
so that even in the fall,
new leaves can continue to unfurl.
It's time to fortify
the foundation,
to bolster the boundaries,
to lavish the love.

FROM: LOVE #109

Thursday, 8 October 2020

Believe it
it's real...
the dissolving of the simulation
to learn Rejection and Humiliation.
You're no longer in the picture,
and your life it getting richer,
feeling lighter all the while,
it's now easier to smile
committing to a new direction
blessed with allies and protection
no need for the validation
of external animation,
but the mirror showing truth
brings the energy of youth
'cuz now you really *are* alive,

and you're learning how to thrive
honoring the women's power
come before you in this hour
calling forth the magic hidden
until now that you've been given.
Learn to build and let it flow,
it will tell you where to go
an'all the ladies with you now
have their version of FemPow!
Sharing in an inspiration
full of faith and dedication
now the world can be transformed
every heart upon it, warmed
this momentum can't be stopped
for tenacity is topped
with a yearning to discover
fear's transmuting into lover.
Hold on loosely, stay aware.
I know that you deeply care,
and I'll be here glowing brightly,
how exciting day or nightly!
Wash those windows, see more clearly,
Love flows to and from you dearly,
unforseen though it may feel,
Believe it now, for it is real.

FROM: LOVE #110

Friday, 9 October 2020

The electric static
of a brain with no sleep
buzzes in short circuits
around your head,
the occasional spark
bouncing randomly
with chaotic rhythm.
Your raw nerves,
shake all the way
to your fingertips,
still holding remnants
of the grief released
the night before.
Grateful for gravity,
that orients you to which

way is up, you pause
in the kitchen window,
sitting on the square black stool,
and watch the squirrels
leap and twirl in playful
spirals. They soften
your beating heart, and
your resolve to persevere
renews itself steadfastly
like a gray rock,
solid, steady,
and ready for another day
with Love by your side.

FROM: LOVE #111

Saturday, 10 October 2020

Come back inside,
into the garden,
where the flowers are,
and the fountain of
Joy flows into the
river of Love, lining
the winding paths
with lush greenery
that lead to the
gazebo in the clearing.
There you'll find the welcoming
company, freshly baked
cranberry scones
with crème fraiche
and hot Lapsong Suchong tea,

bright red strawberries
dipped in dark chocolate,
and chairs with
comfy pillows,
and even a stool
to put your feet up.
You can go back
out again another time.
For now, come pause
with me
in your secret garden.

FROM: LOVE #112

Sunday, 11 October 2020

Floating through the air,
you fall freely
down and down
free-falling,
nothing to hold you
because you just knew you
had to release your grip
on that jagged rock,
and jump into space,
regardless of having
no idea
what would follow.
Scary air surrounds
your fast breathing,
and the fall continues,

as down you go,
falling,
falling,
until you realize,
there's no need to
be afraid.
In mid-flight, you open your heart
and feel the air rushing by,
aware of the void beneath,
the void you are in,
and settle into the spacious movement,
with faith that something
miraculous will soon take place.
And even if it doesn't,
you will already have
experienced the miracle through
your own anticipation of it,
and through the faith and love
filling your heart
in the present moment.

FROM: LOVE #113

Monday, 12 October 2020

The big soft fluffy pillow
that caught you
this morning
cradled your landing
in a blessing
through the phone lines
from across the miles
and through blood
of a different kind.
It's a life line that
resonates with Goodness
and bravery, vibrance
and solidarity
through pain and
grief, loss or struggle.

Bigger than, yet
encompassed in the
miraculous Divine details you opened to
and are playing out now,
it's providing a whole new room
for living, for genuine intimacy.
Inside this invisible room, there's
room to breathe
room for expression
and spacious room for
invisible beauty
invisible quality
invisible love.
It's invisible,
though very palpable
if you're paying attention
and open to its magic.

FROM: LOVE #114

Tuesday, 13 October 2020

This day you wake to a wall of anger
with its spiky edges.
It is not the first of its kind.
But this is a new day,
because the re-wiring
you've been doing
set the spark, not to heat
that wallowing soup of
helplessness,
stuck cooking behind the towering wall,
but to create an appetizer of change,
a brand-new motivation
linked to a fierce determination
to find the way out
for good...

or maybe the way over,
or the way through.
Regardless,
it matters not how you get out,
but that you have transmuted
the crippling anger into
useful fuel.
The power within and
linked to without
is now shifting its focus,
honing in
on its deeper why,
your deeper why.
Your dreams are meant to live.
This is the pilot light
that is serving to
ignite the bigger
fire of truth and transparency
calling you
to serve others in hearing
their own muffled voice
that, like yours, had been
muted
until now.

FROM: LOVE #115

Wednesday, 14 October 2020

Although the vortex
has been howling
around and through
you, and at times
it has even felt like
giving in to its
familiar magnet
would make it all go away,
you can no longer
pretend not to notice
the emerging
rhythm your body
would rather dance to,
the one that is coming
out of the rubble

of the structures that
are collapsing under
the pressure of the wind.
The release of the
energy once held
in these crumbling walls
creates havoc because
it knows not where to go.
But this chaos is only
serving to clarify the
voices that remain steady,
the ones that can hold
a conversation, the ones
that understand the magnitude
of the love needed to hold
all of this flying pain.
Stay connected
to the Love side.
This is where
the steady is.
This is where your
friends are.
This is where
you are

at your
best.

FROM: LOVE #116

Thursday, 15 October 2020

Just like the wind
inspires a sailboat
to move,
I offer extra
fuel for your engine,
as you bounce from
doctor to doctor
with your Mum and
her mysteriously
swelling wrist,
like a balloon slowly inflating.
Hours and hours
go by
and onward you
go, blessed with

humor and patience,
energized by
Love from within.

FROM: LOVE #117

Friday, 16 October 2020

What a joy
to plant new seeds
of abundance
under this new moon.
Instead of
the rigid fence of
control,
they will surround you
by a rich imagination
that expands with
each day, and opens
to the plenitude of
a flourishing
life.

FROM: LOVE #118

Saturday, 17 October 2020

Expand yourself
into the openness
you had renounced
from Guilt's guidance.
The collapsing into
the self that had
once served as protection
is making it harder
and harder
to breathe.
Go easy and gentle
with the deep inhale
of Love for this day
so that the relaxation
into alignment

can naturally
fall into place.
There now,
Breathe,
slow and steady,
into your heart.
She is the excellent
guide you have
been looking for.
And I, Love,
am her mentor
so that you may be
nurtured
on all levels.
Try it out.
See for yourself.
The choice is
yours.
We are here.

FROM: LOVE #119

Sunday, 18 October 2020

As you awaken to
the rays of sunshine
peeking through
the trees,
and the crystal in your
East-facing window
transforms their yellow light
into rainbows across
your bedroom walls,
the birds chime and chortle,
and the day unfolds
its beginning
with a beaming blessing
of breath

and its gift
of Life.

FROM: LOVE #120

Monday, 19 October 2020

You have carried enough.
Wracked with guilt
for your desire to
break free
and for the clarity
you see, it feels
as if your very being
were betraying
the system that
claims to love you.
But what "love"
fills you with such self-doubt
and hesitation to speak,
so much stress to get it "right"
and fear of rejection,

fear of your own anger
and wondering if you'll
be able to protect yourself
gracefully *this* time?
And who will hurt who?
What is this "love" that has you
striving for unattainable perfection
when you are already perfect
as you are.
What "love" uses praise and money
to control you,
and humiliates you effortlessly
in front of others.
What "love"
pressures you to disregard
your own feelings.
This "love" can't hear you
or hold a place for you in your wholeness.
It's accepting only the parts of you
that it approves of,
minimizing what matters to you,
and driving you to contract,
be silent,
disappear...
or sometimes bringing you

into overwhelming
reaction, rage, resentment
that you then need
to tame in turn.
The inordinate
effort it takes to stand here
brings no joy.
It infuses crazy.
No wonder you're confused,
exhausted.
The crumbs they toss
in your direction
do not nourish you.
Nor, it seems, do you
nourish them.
The sleepless nights
offer no solace, no rest.
The loops of rumination
only make you dizzy,
and do not help you grow.
This is your training
ground,
and now you have grounded
wisdom in what

Love
is not.

FROM: LOVE #121

Tuesday, 20 October 2020

I'm holding you gently,
holding you still,
not to control you,
but to soothe
the agitation that
has settled into
your bones
and raised your hackles
all up your spine.
The wild one inside is
snarling to protect herself,
thrashing and screaming
because she is startled, frightened,
awakening
from a long, dark nightmare

she thought was real.
What if we all cuddled
together under this
cozy blanket of Acceptance
with pillows of Kindness
on a bed of Love?
Could we rest then?
Could you find a way
to forgive yourself
for what you still need
to learn?

FROM: LOVE #122

Wednesday, *21 October 2020*

Even if for now, you're
untangling the contortions
you have twisted yourself
into, like one of those
balloon animals
at the fair,
even if all you can feel now
is a ripping pain
because you are puzzling
through how to loosen
the knots that
are gnarled with others,
even if it hurts now,
this is not a new pain.
Rather it's one you

hadn't met yet,
held fast in
these rigid poses
for so long,
and melded into
the expectations
of the circus master
to keep the show
going on.
Even though the untangling
hurts now, it will
open the circulation
back up, and
give your balloon
a new opportunity
to create its own shape
and maybe even
make shapes with others
one day.
But first,
get the knots out
and free yourself
from the other balloons.
PS: Good thing you're a sailor,
and you're good at knots!

FROM: LOVE #123

Thursday, 22 October 2020

Expanding
into this
vastness of
spaciousness
where there is room
for everything in its
purity without imposed
judgment,
my love for you stretches
without losing its
elasticity.
Tapping into your
alchemical powers
and abilities for
transmutation,

you discover hidden
skills enhancing your
capacity to feel,
without losing your
stability.
Releasing the addictive junk food
of drama, shame and guilt,
you open to a whole new
potential for your brilliance
to shine, without shedding
your humility.

FROM: LOVE #124

Friday, 23 October 2020

Here we are together,
in this world
between worlds,
as if landing
in a smooth lake
after making it
through the tumultuous
rapids of the river
that brought you
here.
Moving through the
still waters with a
pleasant surprise
of gratitude that
you still have a

vessel to travel in,
you are reminded that
your good vessel is indeed your
most loyal companion
and a devoted guide
that offers you deep wisdom.
The air smells different
here, and has a lightness
that allows you to breathe
deeper.
Through the calmness of the
forest, you can hear
the smallest bird singing.
Breathe.
Just breathe.
Breathe in the miracles
of your senses,
letting them adjust
to a new landscape,
while touching base
with this new
Fun-loving discernment
pointing your way
to your Destiny.

FROM: LOVE #125

Saturday, 24 October 2020

As much as your body
feels the growing anxious tightness of
this new aloneness
you're tapping into,
I know
your panic is only
physical withdrawal
of sticky habit.
The waxing moon
your eyes landed on
as you looked to the sky
attests to the reflection
of warm light
that grows day by day
and the unquestioning presence

of Divine company.
I am still with you,
and I offer comfort
on a grander scale
to chew up the panic
and spit it out,
so you can rest
assured the only
things that are
expanding
are the moon,
the Universe,
my Love,
and you.

FROM: LOVE #126

Sunday, 25 October 2020

The clunky old thick
metal of your spaceship,
with all its
bolts and washers,
and extra layers,
one inside the other,
seems to be disappearing
with each day you wake.
Some pieces slip off unnoticed,
perhaps quiet because
they land in the soft grass
on your walks
or float into the stars
as you sleep,
while others clank and clatter

or hang off sideways
in an encumbering manner
until you shake them off
deliberately.
This morning you woke
to a streamlined shape,
elegant and simple,
of shimmering dark
metallic blue, with
flowing curves and
minimal protrusions,
made to hover, dash,
swerve or cruise.
Tough as a diamond
and light as carbon fiber,
I offer you a new ship.
"What does this have to do
with Love?" you ask.
With its lightness you will
have less to carry, less to repair,
less to keep track of,
and less to distract you.
With its strength you will
have more effective protection,
ability to resist, and power to persevere.

It will enhance your journey
in unpredictable and
beautiful ways because
it is a shape-shifter,
like me, and will travel
nimbly in any landscape,
or in any direction
of quantum space time.
You are free to explore
the world with LOVE,
and the best part?
You can bring
friends.

FROM: LOVE #127

Monday, 26 October 2020

I believe
you have the capacity
to learn to see what
you cannot yet see.
I believe
your heart can learn
to beat a steady rhythm
aligned with Love.
I believe you are
brave enough to
show up in new ways
you cannot recognize.
I believe your old
habits keep you blocked
in boring ways

that bring you down.
Yet I believe you
are not stuck, and
there are options to explore
in very safe ways.
I believe that you
are free to live
to Love
to Laugh
as you wish.

FROM: LOVE #128

Tuesday, 27 October 2020

The little trail
of Love poems that
led you from the
cul de sac of fear
to a little mountain
with a beautiful view
is now calling you
to follow it
to the open meadow
of wild flowers and butterflies
where the fragrance
of beauty meanders
through the surrounding
trees.
It has taken a new

shape because you
have too, and its
expansion is calling
you to remember
the curiosity of
discovering Love
and the magic
that filled your essence
when you first listened
from that place of
wonder.
This is the delicious food
that plumply nourishes
your exploration
and energizes the potential
you are seeking
to honor,
as you learn what
it means
to bloom forth
in service
to the whole.

FROM: LOVE #129

Wednesday, 28 October 2020

I would like to
celebrate the mess
inside you, because
the guilt and shame,
the self-doubt and insecurity,
the resentment and confusion,
the shrinking and hiding,
the too much not-enoughness,
the anger blown to rage,
the fear of loss of control,
the terrified hypervigilance,
the self-rejection and betrayal,
the pain of generations past,
the manufacturing of denial,
and each matching mask

outfitted to present
a "better" side,
as well as the humiliation
of having all of these
present in one being,
is not unique to you.
I'm celebrating your
willingness to turn the light on
to see your own
beautiful mess –
the only invisible mess
you can actually
clean up.
You have dropped your
judgment and opened
your heart,
and what will define you
is not your particular
mix of these ordinary illusions,
but where you go from here
with each decision
you make.
In this experiment
of Life,
you get to learn

to love your own messy insides,
and their warped
adaptation for
survival,
and see how they transform
on their own
from this Love.
As you do,
You build the capacity to love this
in another
and to lead them
into Love.

FROM: LOVE #130

Thursday, 29 October 2020

Even though tonight is chilly,
there is a golden warmth
emanating from your
shining heart
that you have never
felt before.
The melted caramel
sensation of relief
from the clenching ice
in your chest
brings with it dreams
of sweet softness
and tasty love.
Could it be that you
have found the kind

of treasure that,
like a spring,
is of endless
value?
Drink it in,
for now is when
the magic is alive,
and your resilience
is just beginning
to find its bounce.

FROM: LOVE #131

Friday, 30 October 2020

Isn't it interesting
that as you sit comfortably
in your new Living Room
of Acceptance,
snuggling on your Malibu blue
couch you got in anticipation
of visitors,
the one who showed up
today is Forgiveness.
She waltzes in gracefully,
her emerald robes
flowing gently around her,
and greets you with a
knowing smile
and twinkling brown eyes.

"I'm your new friend,"
she declares, as
she winks at Acceptance, who is
reclined in the gold-striped wingback chair.
And, you notice, she
adds a wonderful flair
to the unexpected delight
that surprises
can bring.
"Just in time for the graduation
preparations,
for our afternoon celebration
of Love and Abundance!" you coo
in your welcome.
"Oh, I love Abundance!"
Forgiveness lights up.
"She collaborates so readily
with anyone who will
open to her. And Love,
well, she's magnificent!
We often all work together –
it's so much fun!" She laughs,
as if recalling
a particular success.
This fresh boost of

lively energy reminds you
of the supplies you
want to get for the
Full Moon party.
But presently you jump
to your feet and invite
us all to join you
to cast your
new voice
for the first time in person,
in a vote
down at the Court House
as one precious voice
among many.

FROM: LOVE #132

Saturday, 31 October 2020

My dear precious soul,
Clear Daughter of the Stars
who lives on the River of Swans,
you are right where
you need to be,
in the here and
now,
at the intersection
where the vertical
of sky and Earth
cross the horizontal
of ancestors and descendants,
the sweet spot
landing right in
your strong vulnerable heart.

This spot is where
the wisdom flows
and speaks
to the sweet spots
of fellow hearts
also dedicating
energy
to our collective
healing,
our collective flow,
our collective story.
You are not alone.
You are loved.
You belong.
You are a valued part
of the whole,
Just like everybody
else.

FROM: LOVE #133

Sunday, 1 November 2020

Sometimes it's hard to look back.
Sometimes it's hard to look forward.
Sometimes it's hard to look in
the mirror
and see the distortions
you create for yourself
as a means of
protection,
when the best salve
is to see with open
eyes of Love and
compassion where you are,
so you can navigate
and move your own
boat better,

even if it is just
a row boat.
You have a place
for Safety beside
you, although
I know you are
suspicious.
What if, just like
you had a different
impression of me,
you could open your
curiosity to Safety?
You might discover
you have another
new friend.

FROM: LOVE #134

Monday, 2 November 2020

I know you don't
want to write today;
the feelings of
numbness circle
around and around
the dense blocks
of stuckness.
And the steadfast
determination to stay there
shuts your ears
to even want to hear
from me.
It's hard for you to
believe me
and see beyond

the silence.
I'm still here,
and I'll go on a walk
with you in the moonlight.
You can sit on
the bench overlooking
the graveyard,
with the rivers joining together
under the rising moon beyond,
and wonder what you
are doing here,
struggling to utter
the words,
"It's ok for me to live."
Then winding your way
down the hill
through the night woods
and down the stone stairs
'til you reach the bottom,
you find the
magical sign that says,
"A Journey of 1000 miles
starts with one step."
and then,
"Start your journey Here."

You smile to yourself.
So, this is why the land
called you here.
Here at the confluence
the parts integrate
into one, with
the promise of
wholeness built
from a fractured past
that parallels not only
your story,
but this land's and
this town's story too.
It carries the unity of
consciousness itself,
so that through
your participation in life
in the now,
while you ARE alive,
you can start to live your story
as you,
and that is
enough.

FROM: LOVE #135

Tuesday, 3 November 2020

"What would it be like
to be the river
below the confluence,
where the merging
has already
happened, and
integration has created
a more formidable river,
broadened to include
all the waters
from each source?"
you ask.
"What would it
be like
to be the banks

that embrace
the powerful waters,
expand to receive them,
and guide them to
their bigger ocean
in the East?"
you wonder.
You are discovering,
in your own nascent wholeness,
what it is to be both
the growing river
that gathers
its streams,
and the riverbanks and bed
that hold its dynamic
presence.
It is in being both,
and in this natural
state of unfolding,
that you enter the
void of creation
where you can experience
being more
consistently
magic.

FROM: LOVE #136

Wednesday, 4 November 2020

My Dear Child,
The Good is in you.
It never left.
It is why you sit
and listen to the
stars and hear
of glory in its dignity
opening to new
worlds of beauty
surprisingly revealed
only through simple
stable doors.
The Goodness you
seek is not beyond,
but within

your inside world,
if only you will
open your brilliant eyes
again to see.
Despair not for
what has passed
but release it
gently with your
mourning. The time
has come to
welcome the adventure
that awaits you,
the unknown joys
and companionship
of tales yet untold
in which each chapter
gets better
and better.

FROM: LOVE #137

Thursday, 5 November 2020

As simple as bread
and butter or
rice 'n miso soup,
or grilled cheese and carrot
sticks, or French
fries and mayonnaise,
or chips and salsa, or
churros con chocolate,
or strawberries
and cream, or
pancakes and maple syrup,
I love the idea of
you and me, together
forever,
Amen.

FROM: LOVE #138

Friday, 6 November 2020

First thing to happen
today, after the
plants get their
thirst quenched,
is a solid dose of Love for
you.
Hard for you to pause
and open to receive
it, you have spread yourself
in so many directions
that may all be
leading to
the same North Star,
but nonetheless
are flattening your

presence to a
pancake.
I'm adding in home-
made maple syrup,
boiled with Love
down to its essence
of dense delight
while maintaining
the pure energy of
life that flowed
through the tree
that bore it,
and inviting
you to the party
of pleasure and
companionship
of glorious design,
bold flowers and luscious
fruit.
Let the sun shine
in your heart
today and illuminate
your way,
so that the next first
thing to happen,

includes love
for you.

FROM: LOVE #139

Saturday, 7 November 2020

I love you.
It's clear.
You're precious
and dear,
expanding
to hold
your presence
so bold
if only
you knew
your value
like dew
it quenches
my thirst
with droplets

a burst
of pleasure
and calm
with grace and
aplomb
still striving
with steady
big Love
at the ready.

FROM: LOVE #140

Sunday, 8 November 2020

OY! Chispita!
What is this
cranky agitation
irritation.
Could it be you're
just dehydrated?
Here is a tall
silver bottomless
cuppa LOVE
for you to drink
to your
heart's content,
with free refills
at the Bar
of Plenty.

FROM: LOVE #141

Monday, 9 November 2020

Today it's a haiku –

In the spirit of
efficiency, I love you
Today and Always.

FROM: LOVE #142

Tuesday, 10 November 2020

As the bow of
the Sarah Effie
plows through the water
and the sunshine
warms your back,
maybe the
gurgle of the
waves breaking along
the hull
can rock you
gently and settle
the anxious nerves
that have been
bouncing around,
screaming for

attention.
There is safety
outside of holding
the vows.
You have
a place.
It's ok that
you're free.

FROM: LOVE #143

Wednesday, 11 November 2020

The foundation
of Presence that
continues to solidify
offers further clarity
for discerning
decisions that lighten
the load and
allow the pace to
soften. It opens more
space for breathing
and a chance to anchor
deeper inside,
where stability lives,
because the reference points
outside are now shaky

and unreliable.
A doorway opens
into Simplicity,
and you don't
hesitate to walk
into the dazzling
beckoning elegance
on the other side,
without any need
to look back,
without a trace
of regret.

FROM: LOVE #144

Thursday, 12 November 2020

I wonder if you
can hear me –
It seems as though
you are in a cloud,
a spongy cloud
that swallows my
words before they
can reach you.
Maybe I'll just
hold you, like a blanket
would hold a baby,
and rock you to sleep
as I tell you a dreamy
story of magic and honor,
bravery and valor,

gold and glitter.
Since you have heard
the tale many times before,
it may still reach
you in your rainbow dreams
and remind you
that you too have
great potential
to shine.

FROM: LOVE #145

Friday, 13 November 2020

Just as the air is
getting colder and the
rain and wind whisk
the leaves off the
trees, you feel
the stir inside
to shift into a
new season.
The parties were
festive while the
enchanted juice flowed
and Denial entertained
the crowd with jokes, but
now that they are gone,
you find yourself with

the heavy Sorrow and
anxious Guilt that had
been playing the music
in the background, barely
audible under the din of
the ruckus laughter.
Now their melancholy
melodies swirl around
without distraction,
and they tug at your
chilled heart, whaling,
"Please don't leave us!"
Their calls are magnetic,
as they are like old friends,
and you've welcomed their company
so that they have begun to
think that they belong here.
They've had their fun,
but their kind of fun
has made holes in your boat,
leaving you exhausted
at the end of each day,
trying to stay afloat.
Follow the seasons, and
let these weary guests

go with the dying leaves.
In sending them
on their way, you
might find a natural
warmth well up to
fill the holes and stop
the sinking, and a
quietness that allows
you to tune in to your
own song. You
could even invite a
new band to
play with you.
As a start, you might
like the lead vocals.
I will play the bass.
I hear that Joy
is a skillful
drummer...

FROM: LOVE #146

Saturday, 14 November 2020

The emptiness
that you have been
attempting to fill
with cheese and crackers
and clams and
shrimp and olives
and wine
has nothing to do
with your stomach.
It's an emptiness
so deep, carved out,
like the Chesapeake Bay itself,
by the meteor
of truth that has
blown through your

world and rearranged
your inner landscape
in unrecognizable
ways.
It's an emptiness
that allows you to
touch your essence
as everything else
has been pretty well
stripped, but there
is a nakedness
that feels cold in
the November air.
It's a void at the
edge of potential,
a simplicity of presence
that you are not
accustomed to, so you
think something is
missing.
But you are whole
again,
full like the moon
and bright like the stars.
And as you allow your core

to flourish, you'll find
that what you thought was
emptiness is
actually a spaciousness
of plenitude in which you can
breathe most freely,
because the possibilities
in *that* place
are endless.

FROM: LOVE #147

Sunday, 15 November 2020

What has you
so closed, like a
clam in the mud?
Is it that you are
afraid you might
get sent back, as
returned merchandise
that didn't quite fit?
Do you actually believe
I would let you go
now that I have gotten
even just a glimpse
into your glowing heart?
I sit on a sandy beach,
with wavelets lapping

their greetings of
gentle salutation
in hopes that you will
hear the whispers of
love meant for you.
You sit with me,
the ache in your heart
longing for some
reflection of what
it might feel like
to share the sunrise
with another –
someone you could
breathe in,
someone you could
touch, someone
you could kiss.

FROM: LOVE #148

Monday 16 November 2020

Let the salty tears
roll down your
soft cheeks
that they may
find their way
back to the ocean
that lies at the
mouth of the Bay
where you are
crying.
Let the gusty winds
guide you to focus
on the sails you
set, not the gale
that blows

through.
Let the sand
between your
toes remind you
of the connection
you have with this Earth
in all her wisdom, and
let my love
carry off those
burdens you have
been bearing
that are not yours
to hold,
so that in your lightness
you can float up
to the open sky
and see what you *are*
responsible for
from a new perspective.

FROM: LOVE #149

Tuesday, 17 November 2020

While you may
not feel like you
belong anywhere,
or with anyone,
you do belong with me,
right here,
in this place
of perpetual
welcome
that questions not
your needs or
feelings, but
rather seeks to
understand them
and uncover

with you
the simplicity
of what lies
underneath –
the power of
your inner wisdom,
and the enticing you
you might
find by being
true to
your own heart.

FROM: LOVE #150

Wednesday, 18 November 2020

Somersaults and
handstands
flip the script
and add a touch
of play, inviting
a different kind
of core to hold
the conversation,
because love
comes in body form
too. I sense the
giggly joy that
bubbles up to
greet the new moon
in anticipation of the

waxing hopes and
dreams you are just
starting to believe
might be possible,
and I wonder
how I will find creative
ways to surprise
you with the support
you need so that
you know I am
here, doing cartwheels
for you.

FROM: LOVE #151

Thursday, 19 November 2020

I hear the voice
that's coming
through from inside
the depths and
has been hiding
for fear of
annihilation.
I hear your bravery.

I hear you pleading
for support,
for someone to listen,
for guidance,
for love.
I hear your vulnerability.

I hear that same
voice reaching
across the abyss
of fear to build
a bridge of trust
with new engineers
who eat courage
for breakfast.
I hear the love.

I hear you, brave one.
I hear you, vulnerable one.
I hear you, loved one.

FROM: LOVE #152

Friday, 20 November 2020

The freight train that
arrives through your
head is not the
same one that usually
travels
down by the river.
This one comes
through unexpectedly
and drops you to your knees
at the porcelain bus.
It's a surprise journey
that flattens you
horizontally for the
remainder of the
day, drifting in

and out of dreams and
more stories of travel.
But you don't go
anywhere on this
trip. Instead,
it's an invitation
to stop altogether,
to listen and rest,
to breathe
and do nothing.

Re: tremendous migraine of new dimensions

FROM: LOVE #153

Saturday, 21 November 2020

You awaken with
delicate movements
as you notice the
lingering pain in
your aching head.
Love today will entail
an isolation into
softness, pausing
into stillness, and
relishing the quiet
space of gentle
warmth.

FROM: LOVE #154

Sunday, 22 November 2020

Just like a
Beautiful precious
shiny ball of love,
oozing with
sparkle and playful
twists of evolving
discovery, and morphing
by the moment
into new shapes,
you are honing in
on an authenticity
that flexes as
you grow
and becomes
more like home

with every
decision
you make.

FROM: LOVE #155

Monday, 23 November 2020

As melodious
as a blackbird,
you sang your song
bravely from the
rooftop of your being,
gliding through the
conversation as gracefully
as a swan on glassy water,
and sharing deep care as
tenderly as a cockatoo,
while maintaining the
sovereignty of a quetzal,
the elegance of
a blue heron in flight,
and the camaraderie

of wild geese in formation.
You flew across
to the other side
of the river,
where you landed
with the faith
that you can in fact
experience love
in connection
with others.

FROM: LOVE #156

Tuesday, 24 November 2020

The fierce rage
that catches flame
from the spark of
new awareness
ignites an entire
forest of old growth
trees. Trees that
carry extended
memory and intricate
connection between
them, yet are
growing crooked
from the toxic
soil they have
rooted themselves in.

Some have lost branches,
others are missing leaves.
Birds are no longer
building their nests there.
There is no water
pure enough to clean
their roots unless
you count liquid
love. This is
the only gold
that can withstand
the heat of the
explosive fire,
because the tears
you shed at the
loss of the trees
will have no power
to save a single one.
You collapse
with the grief,
allowing it to course
through your own
branches and follow
its natural curve.
Who knows what the

forest will look like
tomorrow.
It's not up to you
to decide which
tree, if any, will
live. The helplessness
melts with powerlessness
to form a new
precious metal:
Surrender.

FROM: LOVE #157

Wednesday, 25 November 2020

Untangling the knot that once was
presented to you as Love –
made up of the sticky cords of
enmeshment, the rigid
ropes of guilt, and the
thorny stems of pain,
you find a golden
line of prestigious
strength. It's the
only one that is
hefty enough to hoist
your sails of freedom, and
the only one that
aligns with a future of
vast possibility. It's

the golden line
of pure love in its
plenitude, and it's the
only one you actually
need on your boat.
All the rest are no
longer necessary.
They won't enhance
your navigation. They
won't offer better steering.
They won't even help you
trim your sails. They will
just trip you up and
mess with your compass.
Now that you know they can
be separated out, you
can sail with greater precision,
greater creativity, and
greater aspirations.

FROM: LOVE #158

Thursday, 26 November 2020

On this day of
Giving Thanks,
I extend my
gratitude for your
visits on the
daily, the sincerity
with which you open
your heart,
and the continued
curiosity that finds
portals I didn't even
know were there,
and I am Love!
I am everywhere!
Yet we are still

discovering new places
together, so it keeps me
coming back too.
I feel an intriguing
combination of welcome
and freedom,
wisdom and innocence,
and a powerful
sense that through
these visits you
are finding more
room to breathe,
to speak, to bounce,
to trust my presence,
and to trust your own
too.

FROM: LOVE #159

Friday, 27 November 2020

Sometimes I offer
a warmth
of comfort, like the
lavender bath in
the morning or the
conversation with
your dear old friend.
Sometimes it's a flurry
of serendipity through
the details of uncanny
precision, magical
appearances and wishes
come true.
And sometime I like
to serenade you

with remarkable music
in the language of dreams,
where no matter
what has happened,
there is always a
space for hope.

FROM: LOVE #160

Saturday, 28 November 2020

I'm here with you to
sing the sea shanty
of freedom.
Even if there isn't
one yet, I'll make
one up just for you,
with a chorus of
Love and verses
of rhyme, and
a melody so enticing
you can learn it
in a heartbeat.
It's time to jump
ship, even if it
means walking

on water, even
if the storm is building.
The safety will come
in the freedom, the
nurturing in the
navigation, and you will
recognize yourself
through the courage
it takes to chart
your new course
and your willingness
to put yourself
at the helm of
the boat that was
meant
for you.

FROM: LOVE #161

Sunday, 29 November 2020

Does it surprise you
that not only do you have the
awareness of a zebra
who senses the presence
and power of a hungry lion,
you also have developed a capacity
to step out of that striped skin to
see that power has its
own energy and comes in
many forms? That,
when you look closer,
not all who are powerful
are predators, and not
all who are prey are weak.
Not all power is scary,

and not all surrender is painful.
It is in this connection
to love and integrity
that you have found
yourself in a field of
discernment where you
know now that the difference
between powerless and powerful
is not in the role you play,
but in the quality of alignment
with that role, and
alignment to the purity of
life itself.
Dominance by another
with the sword of fear,
gives way to a power within
with the wand of love,
and brings you the option
to welcome in power of
a whole new form. With it,
you can expand
with its magnificence,
and learn to recognize
it in another, while altering
your experience in

unprecedented ways
in the world at large.

FROM: LOVE #162

Monday, 30 November 2020

It's as if the notes had been
sleeping, and
through the touch
of the ebony and ivory
they are coming
back to life.
Like a bulb that
is being watered after
a dormant season,
the first
leaves are peeking
out, as it remembers
what it means to bloom.
This slumber lasted
for years, but your

sleepy fingers wake
their way across the keyboard
as if unfolding a
piece of crinkled paper
to see once again
what music had
been written there. The
joy of the renewed
connection flows
freely with the
realization that you
can do this because it's fun.
No pressure. No lessons.
No expectations.
Instead, you can just
savour the pure
pleasure of play.

FROM: LOVE #163

Tuesday, 1 December 2020

As you extend
the foundation of
your sanctuary
in creative ways,
I'm grateful to
have been there
from the beginning
because you are including
me in your decisions,
weaving me into
conversations, and
giving me a place to
rest, to breathe,
to flourish.
Thank you.

FROM: LOVE #164

Wednesday, 2 December 2020

I see the unexpected sorrow you feel
from having lost a precious, playful
little friend today.
Swirling in gray and white, images
of her flash through your chagrined
mind as you reckon
with the idea that she is
gone. You will never
see her again, at least not in
squirrel form, now that you
have buried her rigid body
with fur so soft.
Never will you see her
scurrying around at lightning
speed with her friend,

twisting and twirling together,
spiraling up the dogwood tree,
and never will she come
find you at the window,
or eat another thin
slice of pear as you marvel
at the velocity with which
she chews.
But what a precious gift
of joy and wonder she was
while she was here,
and what a blessing
to have met her
at all.
The candle burns
to celebrate her,
and this loving hug I have,
this hug, is for you.

FROM: LOVE #165

Thursday, 3 December 2020

How is it that
when the truth is
spoken now, it rings as
clearly as a bell
atop a carillon tower,
reverberating all through
your body,
as if you can hear it
with more than just
your ears, and it
echoes through your
whole being.
In contrast, the fluff
that is insincerely
spoken is like the

artificial whipped cream
that comes out of the spray
can that at first seems
tasty, but really isn't good for
you. Or maybe it's more like the
shortcut of the nitrous
oxide straight from the can,
that gives you a good
laugh and a quick high, but
is actually
toxic for your brain.
How is it that by
shifting your perception from
just accepting what's given,
to tuning in to what resonates,
and opening a willingness
to actually feel what you're feeling,
you can hear a music
that you couldn't hear
before? You couldn't hear
the bells when you were
dishing up the ice cream sundaes
topped with whipped cream.
But now, you're running
up the stairs so you can

be the one to ring the bells
just so you can hear them,
because now the whipped
cream just leaves you feeling
empty, and the sound
of the bells is more
filling to you.

FROM: LOVE #166

Friday, 4 December 2020

Among the endless
tasks of the day today,
the best decision was the
invitation you made to a new
toy of power, color
and wonder. It brought the
playful and joyful,
practical and wise,
together into one,
embodying all the
fabulous essences
of the squirrel. You
tapped into a surprising
solution, of which, part
will provide terrain

to dig and
bury little nuts
for future times, and
part will reveal untapped
avenues for fun and frolic.
This radical idea
of listening to what matters
to you means you
are uncovering dreams
you didn't know
you had,
and finding the satisfaction
that comes with
acting
on them.

FROM: LOVE #167

Saturday, 5 December 2020

There is a simultaneous
movement out and in
like the exhale and
inhale of a breath,
where, as you release
and let go of what
no longer serves you,
the inhale brings in
fresh new possibilities
and a rearrangement
of how life is falling
into place for you. And as
your shoulders settle
with the exhale, forgiveness
offers a foot massage.

It's time to let it all
go for real, because
deep down you are
so damn curious about
what life would feel
like if you let yourself
go too. What would
you inhale then?

FROM: LOVE #168

Sunday, 6 December 2020

Dear little one,
You are precious.
What you care
about matters,
even if you are three.
You are loveable.
What you wish for
is important,
even if no one is
listening.
You are worthy.
You deserve to
be happy, just like
everyone else.

FROM: LOVE #169

Monday, 7 December 2020

You may have started
writing these poems
just six months
ago, but you are no
stranger to Love. We
go way back, you and
me. Dancing, smiling,
laughing, caring,
loving, touching
kissing, celebrating.
The magnetic presence
of connection has enhanced
your life's beauty. The
festive discovery of
contact has flowed into the

colorful realm of
glowing wonder,
bringing out a part of
you that has been there
from the beginning, who
found her way around
the globe,
is still here now,
and will be dancing
into the future. She
has no time frame
because she is
your essence –
a rich salty essence that can
be summarized in
the large
heart-shaped Pirate
ring of purple glass
you unexpectedly earned
diving off that sailboat's bow
in the moonlight, fully
clothed... a jewel-filled
treasure chest at your
disposal as you came
out of the water. Looking in,

you immediately recognized
the ring as yours. Now,
months later, you see
the conversation it holds
with all of your selves. All
different, but all linked by a
bold, playful, fun-loving,
adventurous, courageous,
brilliant core. And for
the first time today you feel
continuity in your human
life. For the first
time you feel like
you actually could be
invited to participate
in a long-term
future story. For the
first time you are
not on the fringe of your
life, but smack in the
middle of the intersection
between past and future,
between Earth and Sky,
and Love within and without

is extending in
all directions.

FROM: LOVE #170

Tuesday, 8 December 2020

It's almost as if
what started as a
few snowflakes drifting
down quietly has now
morphed into a steady
snow fall. Just like the
confidence you awakened
and opened to started
gently at first,
the more your internal
garden flourishes, as
the benches come in,
the winding path
gets formed, and the
flowers start to bloom,

in turn attracting
the bees and the birds
and all the animals...
the more that progresses,
the more parts of you
want to come home.
Every day the
snow of confidence
accumulates without a
sound, and you find yourself
both in a dazzling winter wonderland
and in a colorful luscious garden
all at the same time.

FROM: LOVE #171

Wednesday, 9 December 2020

The only way you've
been able to
climb down into
the caves that you
have found is that
you have a torch of
Honesty that is holding
the light to truths
you would rather not
know, or you wish weren't
there. Without this light,
you would likely be
swallowed up,
dropping into the
quicksand

of Denial. It's the
cat-like curiosity leading you
forward, holding hands with
Willingness, that knows
that the deeper you go
into the caves, the
wiser you will get,
and the less you try
to control, the freer
you will feel. With
the tears you shed
along the way, your
heart can expand
from the innerstanding
that despite what you
have experienced, and
no matter how
you have responded, you
are worthy of all manner
of Love, of Abundance,
Joy and Forgiveness.

FROM: LOVE #172

Thursday, 10 December 2020

It turns out that
the Rivers that
flow into one
are not only made
of tears of sorrow
and hidden eddies
of grief, cascades of
anger, along
with the debris of
dysfunction, they
are also emanating
with magical delight,
courageous care and
bubbles of laughter,
making it so the

integration of upstream
waters is richer
than you anticipated,
and you are reconnecting
with some parts you
didn't know until now,
and others that you
loved and missed dearly.
And here, in this place
of wholeness, as the
Queen, you are growing
your raft, which works
out nicely, because as
you make your way
downstream, the waterfalls
will continue to grow too.
By the time you get
to the Ocean, you will
have generated
a sailboat.

FROM: LOVE #173

Friday, 11 December 2020

May you fill this
day with Contentment,
allowing yourself the
space to recognize
the shifts of power and
powerful shifts of
perception that have gifted
you back to yourself. The
arduous explorations of
your internal landscapes
award fruits for you
to savour of the
juiciest, freshest,
yummiest kind. You
can welcome in

an empowered contentment,
for it is accompanied
by a deep satisfaction
that you have earned
your peace. You are
learning what it feels
like to experience a safe
sanctuary inside and
out, designed with Love.
Finding within all
of that, there is room
for breathing and
relaxing fully
into your wholeness.
It's an open contentment –
all the way through you.
Knowing you,
this is A
Big Deal!

FROM: LOVE #174

Saturday, 12 December 2020

Cheers to the
spontaneity of
unexpected joy –
two girls driving
around with the top
down, blankets on
your laps and Christmas
Cocktail Jazz echoing
into the dark night
sky. Striving to
catch all the
glimmering houses
on the very
first Harpers Ferry
Holiday Light

Tour, your simple
essence of excite-
ment ripples into
giggles of awe,
reminding you how
wonderous festive
beauty can be,
how you can find warmth
in the cold winter air,
and how special it
is to have a new friend.

FROM: LOVE #175

Sunday, 13 December 2020

Your heart is open.
The shields are down.
You've cleared the field,
You've come around
the bend of fear
that had you thinking
that you weren't worthy
and thus were sinking, into
a world of thick illusion
where you were swimming
in deep confusion.
Yet all along there was your core
who knew that you were made for more.
Your spark would come in fits and starts.
You didn't know your power.

Nor could you see that all your parts
could integrate and shower
the world around you with a LOVE
that you have found inside.
And now you know that it's a gift,
there's no more need to hide.
The fullness of the LOVE you feel
needs no protective shell.
It radiates a glowing light,
and suits you very well.

FROM: LOVE #176

Monday, 14 December 2020

What a pleasure to take
a break from the
diligence and duty,
and bring in a little
spinning, dancing,
stretching, loosening,
spaciousness, culture and
pause. I celebrate
the exploration of balance
as you play with your
intention to integrate all
your lives, to solidify
your sovereignty, and
to open to abundance.
It seems a wise love-move

to continue incorporating
fun and adventure, as they
are where you are
comfortable, and what
got you excited about
living and learning
in the first place.

FROM: LOVE #177

Tuesday, 15 December 2020

This must be one
of those "flat on your
face" days, where
the irritation grows
with the slightest
mishap, where it
seems as though the
light at the end of
the tunnel just got
farther away, and
a palpable tension lies
just beneath the surface,
ready to pounce on
anything that adds
weight to the task

load. It's nothing
in particular, and
everything at once.
It's no one in particular,
and all of us
at once. It's the
illusional stories that
circle around and
remind you of who you
are not, that scream
and shout because
they know you
are about to let
them go. So, Dear one,
let us move towards
who you ARE –
a soul-filled body of LOVE.
And if we shall fall,
then let us fall towards
where we are going.

Re: finding myself at the end with the idea of falling in the direction you're going, inspired by David Whyte's December 13, 2020 session: *7 Vulnerabilities of Giving*

FROM: LOVE #178

Wednesday, 16 December 2020

Hello, I love you.
If you are reading
these words, it is
because you are loved.
You are loved for
who you are, not what
you do, nor what you
think. Your radiance deep
inside is indestructible,
not because
it's hard and impenetrable,
but rather because it's
malleable, adaptable,
brilliant, shifting, alive,
like a lava flow

that doesn't burn, but melts
what is not kindness. The
you I love is
funny and brave,
graceful and caring.
She flows like water down a
riverbed, warms like
fire on a cold night,
nourishes like soil
for the plants, and breathes
LOVE
in and out
of her Being.

FROM: LOVE #179

Thursday, 17 December 2020

It's charming how thick
the wall is sometimes – the one
that keeps good ideas from
coming in, sending those beautiful
ideas that would have you grow
into a bigger you, back
to where they came from. It's
as if it is a charmed wall
because it seems so friendly
in the way it turns the ideas
away. But fortunately, the good
ones keep coming back, and today,
a Queen friend snuck a few
of them past the wall-keeper,
into the garden. They had been

offered before by another ally and
got lost in the rubble, when your
world was still under construction.
And even though the foundational
building and design continues,
maybe you could receive them now.
Today she brought new twists to
familiar tales of your leading love
expeditions with others in unknown
and imaginary internal landscapes –
visions of tears and laughter,
essence and connection, and
effortless flow into a continuation
forward, where you would be
whole and safe, welcome
and valued, and the natural
version of you could expand beyond
the wall and into the Golden Abundance
of life itself. Now *That*
would be charming.

*How is it that with the tidal wave of energy
flowing through right now, the candle flames are
so still?

FROM: LOVE #180

Friday, 18 December 2020

Chilly though it is
tonight, the candle
light through the
snow lantern shines
a bright warmth
of welcome and
flickers a golden smile
your way to let
you know your
grandmother loves you.
She rejoices with
your craftwork in the
snow that she taught
your mum, who then
passed on the generational

love through creativity
to you. The resourceful
simplicity of elegance
winds its way around the
column of snowballs
while the candle, like
a glowing heart, radiates
out a friendly light
into the darkness. By
honoring the women
who came before you,
you are carrying forth
the torch of expressive
beauty, and through
your hands, finding
your own voice
in the conversation.

FROM: LOVE #181

Saturday, 19 December 2020

With every release
and intentional closure
of old patterns and old
beliefs that inspire
the shedding of
another layer that
is not you, the you
I know and love
shines a little brighter.
It is only in this
exfoliation that you
can start to see
your beauty underneath,
and your alchemical
capacity for learning

serves to squeeze
those extra drops of
juice out of the orange
before you send it
to the compost. These
drops too will be
dissolved into your
liquid love and be added
to your pot of gold.
With every layer less
you are more naked though,
and it may take
some adjustment to
recognize yourself now
that you are
becoming more you.

FROM: LOVE #182

Sunday, 20 December 2020

Even when it's time
to close the door, or
say goodbye; even
when you know it's
what you need to do,
you still feel a void
when you sit with
yourself and notice
the missing pieces inside
of you. You will adapt,
again, but for now
there is a sadness that goes with
it, like butter on popcorn,
drizzling into all
the nooks. This is an

old pain of "we will be
better off apart" that
comes with racking
discouragement because
of how many times
these drama re-runs have
played. But there is
comfort in the peace that
has pervaded these final
tests of discernment at the
tail end of this era,
because it means that
even in times of strain,
you have learned to
speak with Love.
You are opening to a new
kind of story – woven
from the beginning
with sustainable Love,
integrity and alignment, so
you won't have to keep
starting over
after more false outsets.
The portal of Love awaits
you, and once you cross over,

you can jump straight into
my arms, knowing I am
a wonderful story teller,
and I will be with you forever.

FROM: LOVE #183

Monday, 21 December 2020

Hi Honey, you're home.
You can feel it in
your whole being as
you tap into the
flow of beauty, of
magic and prayer
that is floating
across the planet from
all the other open
hearts welcoming
in this new time
and celebrating the
potential we are
embodying as
a collective whole.

This unified Love
is like nectar for
the butterfly in
you, while the Grand
Conjunction of the
planets is locking in
the integration you
have been working
towards. You are
whole. You are complete.
You are ready
for what's next.

FROM: LOVE #184

Tuesday, *22 December 2020*

Holy heavy load
of pain and frustration –
that backpack you are
carrying reflects your travels
through the jungle of "people pleasing" –
responsible for what is not
yours and not responsible
for what is. How did the
lines get so thick that
you can't tell one from
the other? How did
you get so convinced that
disrespecting your own
self was a good idea?
No wonder you're mad.

No wonder you're reaching
for your machete to cut
yourself free. But be
careful not to cut off your
legs, my dear one. Keep those
beautiful strong legs that
hold your balance
and allow you to walk and
dance and take you
to where you will find
a clearing to set your
pack down and bask
in my rays of Love.
There, you'll find the kind
of Love that holds
firm, that protects your
dignity, and that inspires
others to shape up
or ship out.

FROM: GUILT

Wednesday, 23 December 2020

You are worthless
without me. I am
the guide you have
been looking for,
because without me
you would be selfish.
Without me, you
might forget your
duties. Without
me you might get
lost in frivolous and
unnecessary activities
like having fun, experiencing
joy, or doing what actually
gives you deep pleasure. You

might even get the
ludicrous impression that
you are free. Free to choose
what you value,
free to listen to yourself,
and you would be
wrong. I know your
only purpose is
to serve others' needs,
and your own dreams
have no value.
I am good for you
because you are
incompetent of
making good decisions
on your own. If that's not
enough to convince you
to behave, I will introduce
you to my friends,
Fear and Judgment. We
will keep you in your
place, where you
belong.

Re: "What does Guilt have to say to me?"

FROM: LOVE #185

Wednesday, 23 December 2020

If I asked you
a question, then
interrupted your
answer to change
the subject back to me,
would you feel
loved? If you
shared a concern
from your heart, and
I ignored it, replacing
it with something
I felt more comfortable
with, would you feel
loved? If you felt a
need to measure your words

for fear of my anger,
would you feel loved?
If I blamed you
for a situation I
created, would you
feel loved?
Hmm, didn't think so.
Good thing you
know that now.
Glad you're catching on.

FROM: LOVE #186

Thursday, 24 December 2020

I am here
here
here
with the still
stillness
where you
where you are
are.
Can you hear the echo?
the echo?
'cho?
A stillness that's blank
that's blank
blank and still
still,

open and in motion
motion
motion
swirling slowly into the
clear clear space. You
notice a rose-gold shimmer
steady in its presence,
as the echo stops.
It sprinkles and whooshes,
like a gentle glittery
wave and tickles
your skin as if
you were glowing from
the inside too. The
air smells of sweet pine,
and warmth fills your
heart. It's me, Love,
I too am opening up.

FROM: LOVE #187

Friday, 25 December 2020

I am here to
fan the little flame
inside you so that
you may have more
light to see with. You are
so easily swayed back
into the darkness, so
afraid of wagging your
tail. You have opened to
just enough Love for
one visit a day, and it
has been a gorgeous
beginning, a beginning
of possibility. You are
already pondering your

next puzzle... how to
Be even more immersed
in love because
you know now that you
are more than just a
visitor to this world of Love,
dear one; you belong
here. The truth is, there is
no need to ration. There is
enough Love for you to *live* in!
All day. All night. There
is enough for you to be immersed
in every moment, without taking
away from anyone else, because
not only is there plenty for you,
My Love, there is a plethora
for others as well. This
is not economics; this is
Love. It's a whole new system.
There is no supply and demand.
There is invitation and acceptance.
There no calculated allocation,
there is only abundant availability.
There is no Tragedy of the Commons,
but rather celebration

in connection, in collaboration. I see
the part of you that has
her head down, kicking
stones along the path of scarcity,
hands in her pants pockets
and feeling deeply alone,
deeply unworthy. But she too
is included in this Love world,
and warmly welcomed into this
invitation of everlasting Love.
Everyone is invited! So let
go of your worries. Allow
me to send out the invitations
so *you* can float into the
miracle of receiving this abundant
flow. All you have to do
is tune into your gentle
heart and listen to which
way your "Yes" leads you
from here.

FROM: LOVE #188

Saturday, 26 December 2020

If only I could
paint music through
letters to take the
shape of a poem,
and send the melody
of virtue through your
heart to create a
new sensation that
might wake you to
a dream deep enough
inside that you could
hear the tune playing
whenever you needed
a magic ally in
times of peril.

FROM: LOVE #189

Sunday, 27 December 2020

The noose tightens
around your throat
as you feel the pressure
that keeps you from
speaking. Nausea
swims in and around
your body as the nerves
pile up one on top of
the other, eager to see
the show. But drama
no longer entices your
heart strings, and patience
watches as it all dissipates
into nothing. This
is not only your story,

but one that has been
passed down from the
cumulative generations
and therefore feels more
daunting. You can witness
it though, and melt it
into your beautiful heart
with blessings
of forgiveness
and Love.

FROM: LOVE #190

Monday, 28 December 2020

Unknowingly, this exploration
started, in part, long ago,
in a far-off land with
another experimentation.
How can you generate
a space between strangers
that welcomes in the truth?
How can you offer a space
that opens to
what lies underneath;
the wild shy creature
that is our true self...
the one who is paying
attention, the one
who knows when you're

sincere. How can you
connect to life from *that* place
that is so alive, so honest,
so pure, and grow from
there? And how do you
do that together?
Your practice with thousands
is now boomeranging
back; offering this
space of safety to you,
where you too can feel
held and celebrated
and honored.

FROM: LOVE #191

Tuesday, 29 December 2020

Today feels like
a potluck of emotions,
where none of the
dishes quite go
together, and there's
a mishmash of hot and
cold, savory and sweet.
The clay throwing
brought back the
importance of always
returning to center,
so that the emotions
could ride their own
waves and you could
be the centered

dish, even if the
food piled on it
was chaotic,
even if you weren't
hungry, even if
the centrifugal force
kept pulling at you
to split apart.

FROM: LOVE #192

Wednesday, 30 December 2020

Seeping in to your
bones, you feel a
slight panic as you
question whether you
can actually be
independent, whether
you can earn your
keep, whether you
really can land on
your feet in dignity,
and with the wisdom
that guides good
decisions. "What if...?"
Your breath quickens
as your body contracts,

and your thoughts get
erratic, bouncing from
one humiliation to the
next failure. But then
you look up, and your
eyes catch the rose-colored
cyclamen blooming on the
counter, her spiral buds
opening with varying succession.
And the "what if…" turns
to wonder, "what if I could
be bold and brave like her!"

FROM: LOVE #193

Thursday, 31 December 2020

I am the pillow for
your heavy sleepy head,
the thick blanket
whose weight is like
a full-body hug,
and the couch that
is long enough for
you to fit, in your
wholeness, so that
you may rest ease-fully
and with satisfaction
for your valiant transmutation
this year. Little
by little, day by day,
like the rising rivers

from the steady rains,
your efforts have
accumulated, and you
can close out this year
knowing you are
loveable and loved,
worthy and valued,
courageous and respected.
Now for the lullaby...

FROM: LOVE #194

Friday, 1 January 2021

Before crossing the threshold,
you look back one last time
at the storm and disruption
that blew through this past year.
There is a surprised relief
bubbling up from having made it
to this moment.
It was not easy.
You've resolutely gathered yourself
together again, after
so many years of being
like a broken mirror,
reflecting a fractured world.
You had split in indecipherable
ways, like an uncrackable code,

so that even *you* couldn't recognize
yourself. It seemed safer
that way…
until it wasn't any more,
because the glue that kept
the mirror together was
drying out and losing its grip.
In the calm of the eye of this past year's
hurricane, the glue gave way,
and you broke open completely.
The mirror disappeared, and
in its place, there you were,
where you had been all along,
inside – as pure and beautiful
as when you were born.
Untouched by any complicated story,
yet connected to all of life,
your wholeness emanated a
simplicity in its radiant essence.
And instead of broken glass around you,
you found gems in your hands,
you found pillows and plants,
sunshine and rainbows,
squirrels and songbirds,
friends and allies, and

best of all, is the blooming of
our marvelous friendship that
has no shape or shade in particular
and comes in every form and color
under the sun. And with this, we
can go forth together
across the threshold and into
the golden landscape emerging
before you.

FROM: LOVE #195

Saturday, 2 January 2021

Despite the winter
chill, your inner garden's
greenery is filling in,
leaf by leaf, and
the warmth of the
lily's fragrance
radiates like a
beacon for other
gardeners to find
their way to this shared
Love space. It's a space
for the kind of Love that
is smooth as chocolate mousse,
simple as a blade of grass,
solid as a diamond,

natural as a flowing river,
resilient like a trampoline,
and bright like
my Love for you.

FROM: LOVE #196

Sunday, 3 January 2021

I know you wonder if
the solitude will ever
melt into community again,
if the electronic hellos
will ever turn into hugs,
if this Love you are
building will carry you
into healthy ways of
being in the world.
We will never know until
you come back into
this moment, the moment
in which the love is alive,
in which you can celebrate
how far you have already

come; in which you feel
the authenticity you have cultivated
within yourself that moves
with you from this moment
into the next.
Grounded in this wholeness
that is so young in
your experience, you
will find this Love
expanding beyond
your dreams
into the Heavens
and here on Earth.

FROM: LOVE #197

Monday, 4 January 2021

Once upon a time
you loathed your
own presence,
feared your own power,
and erased as much
as you could inside,
so you could disappear.
Anything would be
better than being
present. Present to
feel, present to see,
present to connect.
Disconnection was
safety, and emptiness
was normal. Looking

for yourself in the
presence of others, it's
no wonder you couldn't
find you. You were
missing. You had
vanished. The shell
of your body still
moving through the world
operated as if automatically,
programmed to react by
formula – if this, then that.
And even though today
you feel remnants of
this old story in the
thoughts that are circling,
the tightness of your chest,
and the knot in your
stomach, today
you know that is not you.
Today you know that
your heart is opening
to this life, to your life.
And today, I'm in Love
with the real you,
as you are,

right here,
right now,
You.

FROM: LOVE #198

Tuesday, 5 January 2021

What a great relief
for you to know that
you are not special,
that there is nothing
wrong with you, and that
the more you open to life,
the stronger you become.
The less you think,
the more you can hear.
The more you allow the
wisdom of life to flow
through you, the more
support you find, and
the more you can hear
the truth, the simpler

the clarity of what to do.
At first, your powerlessness
seemed insurmountable, but
it is in knowing where you
feel powerless that you can
find your treasures, your
superpowers, your magic
And it is in opening
to yourself that you
have found me.

FROM: LOVE #199

Wednesday, 6 January 2021

It's cold
and it's cloudy,
and the sun is going down,
but you, my Love,
are just warming up,
just beginning
to shine,
and you are walking
towards
a new
horizon.

FROM: LOVE #200

Thursday, 7 January 2021

Off you go, My Love,
may you fly free, may
you rise from your
own ashes, may you
follow the rose petals
that lead you to
fresh air, may you
shine your love
with your whole
heart, knowing that
it will always be
replenished,
and may you
know in the
wholeness of your

being, that the
world needs you
AS You.

EPILOGUE

Before this experiment of listening for what love would say to me each day, my own voice had been so dim inside that I hadn't seen the connection with my lack of sense of belonging. Often, we attribute belonging to where others tell us we belong. But through these conversations with love, I started to see how as my voice emerged, so did my sense of belonging. Belonging becomes a verb. You belong yourself. Belonging is not the same as matching, or fitting in. When you are connected to yourself, only you know where you belong – where you're meant to be, what you need to do, who you need to be with, and when to walk away. It's no one else's place to tell us where we do or do not belong. We can welcome each other, but we each choose where we belong.

With this newly found love voice that brought forth this sense of belonging arose a sense of natural protection. With this voice I could speak up without creating escalation. Did you know, you can bathe yourself, and thus protect yourself, with love by how you speak to another? When we're too focused on who we're speaking to, we exclude ourselves and get defensive, and in turn, when we're too focused on ourselves, we can't hear the other person, and this may escalate tension. In both cases, love calibrates the balance so that you include yourself and the other in your conversation. This consideration can create a sense of safety and calm for you both.

I also learned we have a choice as to what we feel. We may react inside in uncontrollable ways, but we choose where we linger and what we replay, and we have the power to shift it. This affects our interpretations of situations, as well as our interactions with others. It's essential, then, that we start with grace and kindness towards ourselves and go from there. After all, we know our story best, and we are adaptable and creative survivors.

Though this experiment was initially just to get to know Love, I learned how to speak kindly to this self I found inside, how to comfort her and accept her. The beautiful expansion of this has been a blooming capacity to discern in new ways, so that my 'yes's' look different, and my 'no's' do too. They are now more defined by what feels like my true self. In some cases, what I used to say 'yes' to, I now say 'no' to, and what I said 'no' to have turned to 'yes's.' Through this experiment I developed an undivided sense of somebody-ness and dignity. And the 'yes's' and 'no's' were aligning with *that*.

Two hundred poems ago, I was split like the two rivers I lived by – a professional self and a personal self – one inspiring, the other cowering. Through this process the two parts, made of the same water, merged into one river, wound their way into wholeness downstream, and found their way as one to the great ocean. It took me three years to be ready to publish this second round, to let it fully sink in. Now I am literally writing this by the shore of the Atlantic Ocean.

Having started this experiment with trepidation, as a brief coastal adventure, I now wonder what it would be like to boldly set sail on an off-shore voyage, connecting with Love for more than just the time it takes to write a poem. How could Love become a Life Style? How would Love inspire the way one moves through the world, interacts with others and makes decisions? What would it be like to BE in love all day and night too? What if we knew that Love were coming from the inside, and we needn't seek it from another? Wouldn't that make everything simpler, more reliable, more equitable, and more fun?

Through love, I learned about pure power within – not manipulation, power over, or weakness under. Finding my own power allowed me to let go of enmeshment because I no longer depended on others to care for me when that's an impossible expectation and an impossible imposition. I didn't understand how I was holding others captive when I was not letting myself be free.

When a life is grounded in love, it will also be grounded in accountability. We are responseable for the decisions we make and the actions we take, and that gives us power. If you've given away your power for many years, it might feel weird or terrifying at first to reclaim it. You might even be disappointed or ashamed to see what you've done to survive, but once you dive in, and once you get a taste of inner freedom, you start to see how your perception of life expands, possibilities open, and there is room for more meaningful connections with others, as well as new friends. There, you might find it feels good to be you, the real you. It's not an easy process – it takes courage and persistence. I was all twisted up at first, and feeling bad felt more comfortable and safer than feeling good; hiding was preferable to being seen. That shifted as I learned to see myself, to listen to my screaming insides, and to let her be held with love. She calmed; I grew.

Another thing I learned about Love? It's available for and accessible by all, but not everyone wants it. Some are suspicious or scared, like I was at first. Some think it's weak, or mushy. Some like where they are, as they are, and aren't interested in change. Love is a choice.

If you *are* interested in Love, you can open to it, even generate it! The potential is there for each and every one of us at any moment. It's inside you! It's home-made! You get there by letting yourself breathe and by walking a path that feels like you. Listen to you. Honor you. It's not that you're better, it's that listening to you and honoring you is just better *for you* and ultimately better for everyone. When this is done through love and acceptance, by default we are connected to the whole. Being true to yourself clears the space for those around you to do the same in their own way. This way everyone gets to live their best life! We are each an original source of love, and this variety makes us rich.

Related to this variety in people, I also noticed an opening variety in experiences. One of the essential differences I noticed between my perception before and after this experiment is a clarity of how loops of repeated thoughts, interpretations and reactions eventually get boring and therefore crazy-making. The drama plays out in predictable patterns of escalation, and that's why it's so painful. It's the same pain over and over again, and you can't see a way out! Again?! Love, on the other hand, offers insight, surprise, expanded awareness, unexpected learning, fresh energy, integrity, beauty, creativity, solutions, welcome, wisdom and so much more imponderable inspiration. New ways of being and responding emerge naturally. Having said that, love also opens difficult truths, though they are always offered with care and compassion, and always delivered with the utmost respect.

This Love, I have learned, starts inside. Finding the love inside can be elusive at first, so you keep showing up to meet it. It'll find you in surprising ways. It'll be different for everyone, and it will appear in many different places. It might be through something you haven't even tried yet or thought you didn't like. Eventually, it's wherever you can hear yourself best, or feel most natural, most curious, most sincere, most invigorated *from the inside*. Maybe it's just a sense of relief to hear your own voice. Observe without judgment. Notice where you expand and where you contract, or where you relax and where you tense up. Be honest with yourself. Keep exploring and experimenting until you find your spark. And by spark, I mean you. You might be surprised by what calls you and lights you right up.

Poetry for me was like a surprise trampoline to bounce *from*. I didn't like words, especially not English! But it turns out I do like meaning, feeling, and expression, and through this experiment in poetry, I learned that words could express those elements, untethered, unfiltered. This might be obvious to someone who has felt free to express themselves, but it was a new experience for me.

With each poem I caught a little more air, bounced a little higher and went a little deeper. It's a new love I will continue to hone. And, I wonder, from here where will I bounce *to*? Then I wonder, where will *you* bounce with your spark of Love? Where will you find it? And will we bounce together? Love gives me a feeling of being together, a sense of connection, and I like it, so I will continue to explore this vast, beautiful, expansive world of Love. I have a lot to learn still, but I've come a looong way.

Ultimately, we need me as me and you as you! It's way more fun and less confusing than trying to be someone we're not. It's efficient. It's effective. It's how we can best contribute and enjoy participating. My sense is that being ourselves sooner rather than later enhances our quality of life, and diminishes the fear of dying unsatisfied.

As we shift out of old systems based in fear and survival into a new world of connection and collaboration, we can remain in an inner place of stability. And knowing that things could potentially get worse before they get better, we can hold a place for peace inside too, along with Love and innovation, to help us move into new and un-known territory gracefully together.

Love expands with the space we open for it, a place to be experienced and expressed. I didn't know that until I offered it a space to come into, a way to speak. Opening to it every day gave me a chance to start to recognize it, sense its essence, feel its presence. It brought sovereignty of the sweetest kind, comfort for the courage it took to open, reassurance of being valued and understood, and an unexpected connection with joy. And that was in just a couple of hours a day! By extension then, a *whole system* of Love could rock our world in magnificent ways. I am so excited to design and experience a *Life Style of Love*, singularly and collectively, however that may be and wherever it may take me, us. I hope I see you there. I bet it's gonna feel good.

BIBLIOGRAPHY

Carter, Les. PhD. *When Pleasing You is Killing Me: Setting Boundaries with the Controllers in Your Life.* 2018. Print.

Lewis, John and Michael D'Orso. *Walking with the Wind: A Memoir of the Movement.* New York: Simon & Schuster, 1998. Print.

Whyte, David. *7 Vulnerabilities of Giving.* Langley: Many Rivers, 2020. Online Zoom Session, December 13, 2020.